I0473387

This notebook belongs to:

____

Date:

____

Published by Journals For You Publishing

www.ingramcontent.com/pod-product-compliance
Lightning Source LLC
Chambersburg PA
CBHW072213170526
45158CB00002BA/582